THE STORY OF
Saint Valentine

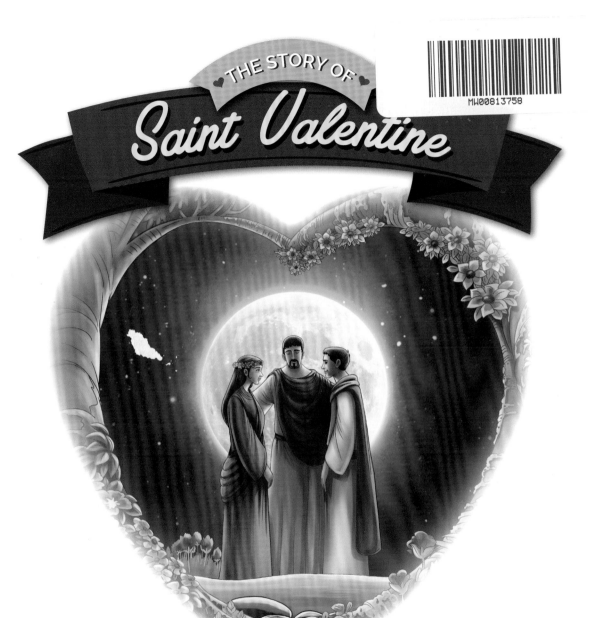

A story of courageous love

Every year on the 14th of February, many people do something very special —they give nice cards or gifts to their friends and people they care about. That special day is called Saint Valentine's Day. But do you know why we celebrate this way and who Saint Valentine was? Let's find out.

3

Many, many years ago, in A.D. 269, the Roman Empire ruled the world —but there was trouble. Enemy tribes were attacking the border. Emperor Claudius II needed to stop them, but he had a very big problem on his hands!

GREAT BRITAIN

FRANCE

SPAIN

ROME

GREECE

TURKEY

NORTH AFRICA

MEDITERRANEAN

EGYPT

The emperor needed a bigger army, but there just weren't enough soldiers to send into battle. He thought and thought about what to do until one day, he got an idea.

"I know what I'll do," he said to himself. "I will send messengers throughout the land to ask young men to join my army. That way I will have all the soldiers I need!"

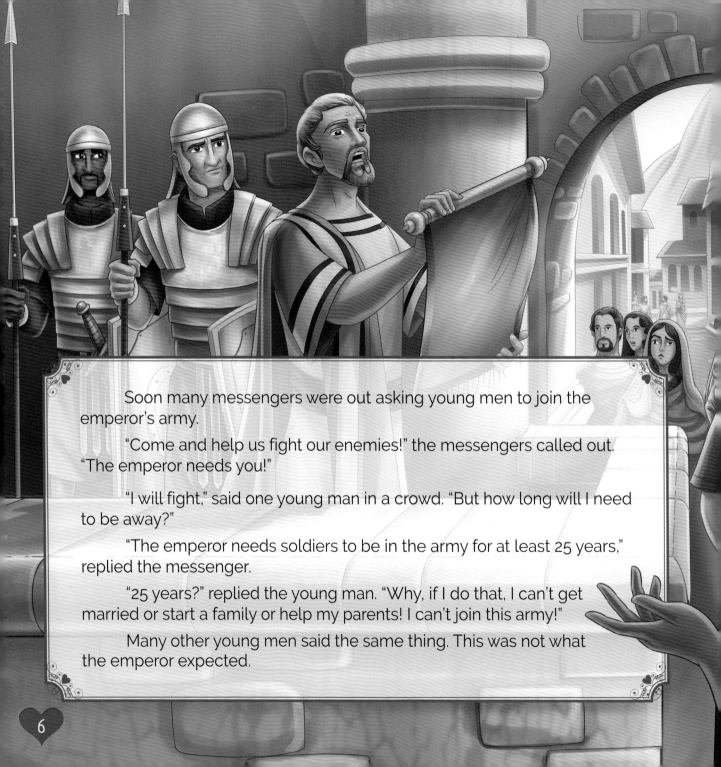

Soon many messengers were out asking young men to join the emperor's army.

"Come and help us fight our enemies!" the messengers called out. "The emperor needs you!"

"I will fight," said one young man in a crowd. "But how long will I need to be away?"

"The emperor needs soldiers to be in the army for at least 25 years," replied the messenger.

"25 years?" replied the young man. "Why, if I do that, I can't get married or start a family or help my parents! I can't join this army!"

Many other young men said the same thing. This was not what the emperor expected.

Weeks later, the messengers returned to Claudius and they looked very afraid.

"How many more soldiers do we have now?" asked Claudius.

"None at all!" replied the messengers, trembling.

"What?" shouted the angry emperor. "How is that possible?"

"When the men found out you wanted them to be in your army for 25 years, they didn't want to join," said one of the messengers.

Claudius became very, very angry. "If the men care more about getting married and starting a family than being part of my army, then I will make a new law!" he shouted.

"From now on there will be no weddings in all of Rome! Not until I get the army I want!"

When news spread about the new law, the people were shocked and very sad. No one could get married in all the land! What could they do?

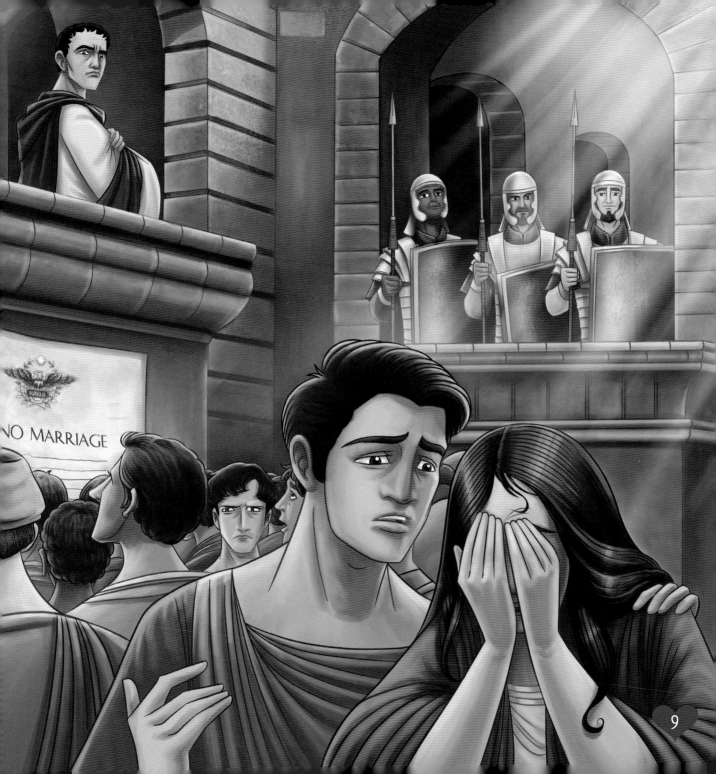

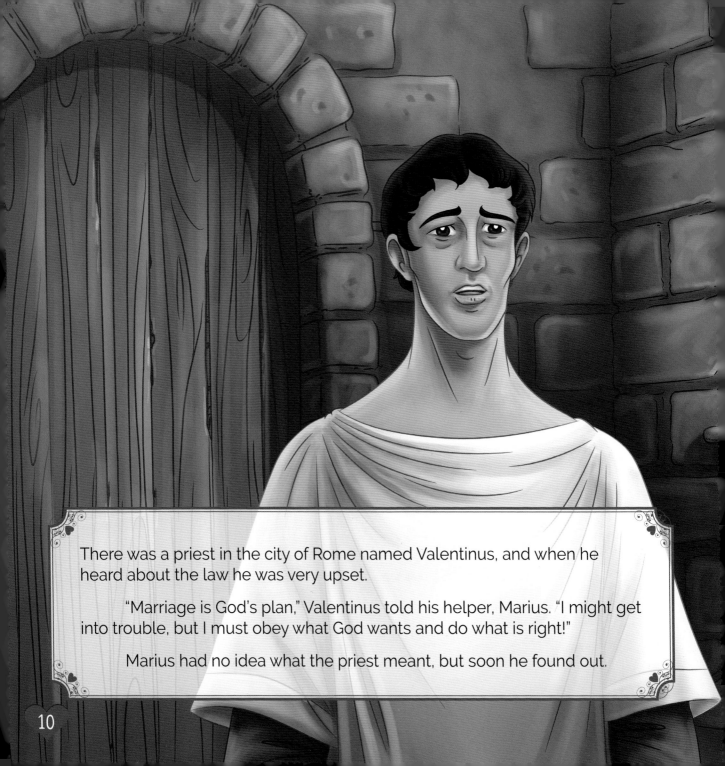

There was a priest in the city of Rome named Valentinus, and when he heard about the law he was very upset.

"Marriage is God's plan," Valentinus told his helper, Marius. "I might get into trouble, but I must obey what God wants and do what is right!"

Marius had no idea what the priest meant, but soon he found out.

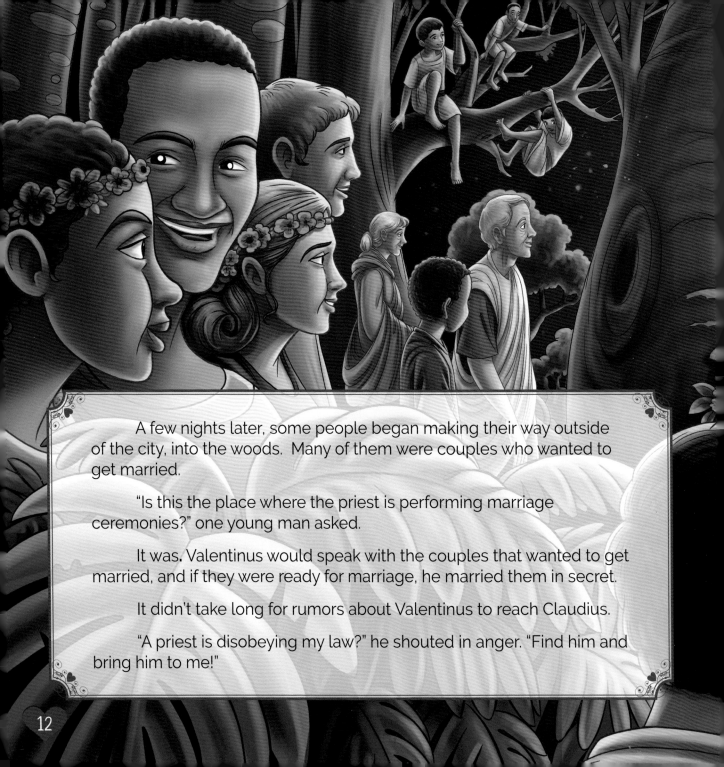

A few nights later, some people began making their way outside of the city, into the woods. Many of them were couples who wanted to get married.

"Is this the place where the priest is performing marriage ceremonies?" one young man asked.

It was. Valentinus would speak with the couples that wanted to get married, and if they were ready for marriage, he married them in secret.

It didn't take long for rumors about Valentinus to reach Claudius.

"A priest is disobeying my law?" he shouted in anger. "Find him and bring him to me!"

Before long, Valentinus was found. Bound with heavy chains, he was thrown at the emperor's feet.

"Why do you disobey my law?" shouted Claudius. "Don't you know I can throw you into prison and punish you?"

Everyone in the room watched Valentinus. They were sure he would beg forgiveness of the emperor. But instead, the young priest looked at Claudius and said, "Marriage is a gift from God. You cannot take that away from the people. If you do, you are disobeying God."

Claudius was surprised at the courage of the young priest and at how much he loved God. For a moment, he even thought about forgiving Valentinus, but then he looked around at the people in the room. "I can't let this priest tell me what to do!" he thought to himself.

Then, in his pride, the emperor shouted, "Take this priest away to prison and have him killed!"

Valentinus found himself in a dark and dirty prison, but instead of feeling sorry for himself, he got on his knees.

"Heavenly Father," he prayed. "Please help the emperor to see how wrong he is. Help him open his heart to You. And please, help the people of Rome."

As Valentinus prayed, the jailer watched.

"What an amazing man this priest is," the jailer said to himself. "How could he be thinking of others when he is in prison?"

Many days later, Valentinus saw that the jailer looked very sad. "What is the matter?" Valentinus asked.

"It's my little daughter," sighed the jailer. "She has been blind since birth and it hurts me to see her like that."

"Don't worry," replied the good priest. "I will pray for her. Let's remember that with God nothing is impossible."

Valentinus' strong faith helped the jailer feel much better.

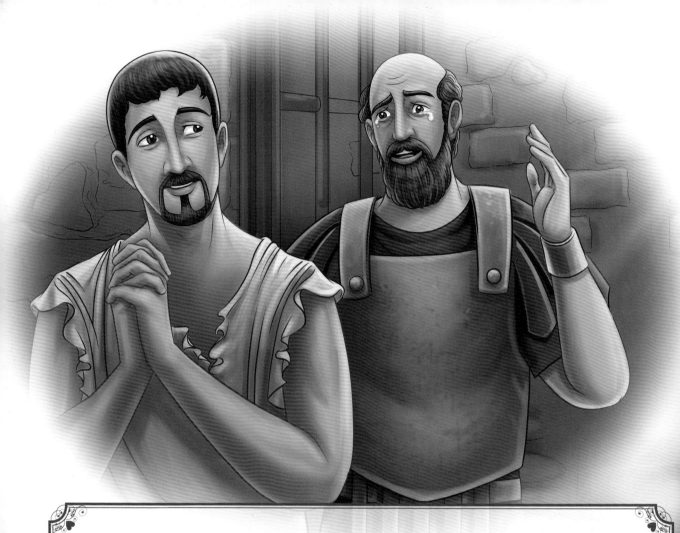

The next day as Valentinus was praying, the jailer ran in.

"She can see!" the jailer shouted. "My daughter can see! It's a miracle! God has healed my daughter!"

Valentinus joined the jailer in giving thanks to God. A few days later the jailer and his family became Christians!

Valentinus taught the jailer and his family all about Christ. He made friends with them and wrote them letters telling them about God's love and he always signed them, *Your Valentinus.*

You are always in my prayers. Remember God loves you.

Your Valentinus

Day after day, the good priest continued to be a brave example of his faith, and people all over Rome were speaking about him.

"What a brave priest!" some would exclaim. "Even in prison he does his best to comfort others!"

"He is a real example of Christ! If he can be such a blessing to others even now, maybe I can, too!"

"I'd like to be just like Valentinus!" some of the children would say. "I want to serve God and be kind and good."

Valentinus' example of humility and love of God encouraged many people to follow his unselfish example. People began to be kinder to each other. They showed more love and went out of their way to help others. Many people came to believe in Christ because of his example!

Even though Valentinus was in prison, he was a reminder that the emperor's law against marriage was wrong. The time came when Emperor Claudius wanted to get rid of him for good. Soon guards came to take Valentinus away.

As he was led outside and away from the city, Valentinus knew the time had come for him to go to Jesus. As he stumbled to the place where he would meet his fate, he prayed: "Lord Jesus, I thank You for the blessing of knowing and serving You. I thank You for dying for me on the cross and filling my life with Your love and presence. I pray now, as I prepare to meet You, please help the people of Rome. Please help more of them to know You. Help them to have faith and to be courageous. Help them to obey You and Your ways. I pray also for the emperor—may he come to know You as well."

"Kneel!" The voice of the soldier that was with him made Valentinus realize that his time to leave this earth had come. He did as the soldier told him and knelt. Then as the soldier lifted his sword, Valentinus prayed one last prayer.

"Receive me into Your kingdom, Lord Jesus!"

And with that, Valentinus, the brave and courageous priest who obeyed God even when it meant prison, was gone.

The date was February 14, A.D. 270.

In 496, Pope Gelasius I made February 14 a feast day in honor of Saint Valentine. Many people began to copy the way he wrote special letters to those he cared about, signing them, "from your Valentine."

So let's remember this good and caring priest the next time we celebrate this special day. May God help each of us be as unselfish and loving as dear Saint Valentine.

"No one
has greater love than this,
to lay down one's life for his friends."

John 15:13

Enjoy your holidays with stories about the people we celebrate:

The Holiday Saints book collection!

Stories of the people whose dedication to God
helped to change the world.

For more books like this one, visit:
www.brotherfrancis.com